Christmas in Victorian Times

Gill Munton

WAYLAND

Victorian Times

Christmas in Victorian Times

Clothes in Victorian Times

Schools in Victorian Times

Streets in Victorian Times

Sundays in Victorian Times

Transport in Victorian Times

How we learn about the Victorians

Queen Victoria reigned from 1837 to 1901, a time when Britain went through enormous social and industrial changes. We can learn about Victorians in various ways. We can still see many of their buildings standing today, we can look at their documents, maps and artefacts – many of which can be found in museums. Photography, invented during Victoria's reign, gives us a good picture of life in Victorian Britain. In this book you will see what Victorian life was like through some of this historical evidence.

Editor: Carron Brown
Designer: Joyce Chester
Consultant: Norah Granger

First published in 1996 by Wayland Publishers Ltd,
61 Western Road, Hove, East Sussex BN3 1JD, England.

British Library Cataloguing in Publication Data
  Munton, Gill
  Christmas in Victorian Times – (Victorian Times)
  1. Christmas – Great Britain – Juvenile Literature
  2. Great Britain – Social life and customs – 19th century
  394.2'68282'0941
ISBN 0 7502 1878 9

Typeset by Joyce Chester
Printed and bound in Great Britain by B.P.C. Books Limited

Text based on *Christmas: Victorian Life* by Katrina Siliprandi published in 1993 by Wayland Publishers Ltd.

Cover picture: A Christmas tree and children's musical instruments.

Picture acknowledgements
Bridgeman Art Library 4, 6 (top); E.T. Archive *cover*; Mary Evans 6 (bottom), 7, 9, 10, 11, 12, 14, 16, 17 (top), 18, 21 (bottom), 22 (top), 23, 24, 25, 26, 27; Illustrated London News 15 (bottom); Mansell Collection 5, 13, 15 (top), 22 (bottom); Wayland Picture Library 19 (photographed by Paul Seheult).

Thanks to Norfolk Museums Service for supplying items from their museums on pages 8, 17 (bottom), 20, 21 (top).

All commissioned photography by GGS Photo Graphics.

Contents

4
Christmas Holidays

8
Christmas in Church

12
Food

16
Cards and Decorations

20
Presents

24
Games and Treats

28 Timeline
30 Glossary
31 Books to Read
31 Places to Visit
32 Index

Christmas Holidays

People who are Christians believe that Jesus was born at Christmas, nearly 2,000 years ago. But most of our Christmas customs only began in Victorian times. That was when people started sending Christmas cards, and getting presents from Father Christmas, or Santa Claus.

Winter Festivals

People have always had festivals in the middle of winter. Even in Victorian times, there were special days for the saints' birthdays as well as Christmas celebrations. Everyone dressed up and gathered together for a party.

This picture shows a winter festival in Tudor times (about 400 years ago). ▼

▲ This Victorian family are playing games and trying out their Christmas presents.

Christmas in Victorian Times

The Victorians began to think of Christmas as a time for families to be together. After 1880, many people in England and Wales had a holiday and could spend Christmas Day at home. In Scotland, Christmas Day did not become a holiday until 1900. Before 1900, children went to school on Christmas Day.

Christmas for Poor People

Very poor people lived in places called workhouses. On Christmas Day, they had a special meal and received small presents. Sometimes, they went to a carol service.

By 1880, even poor children went to school. At school they learnt about how rich people celebrated Christmas.

▲ These homeless people had to spend Christmas in the street.

A Christmas Story

Charles Dickens wrote a book called *A Christmas Carol*, which was published in 1843. It was about a man called Scrooge who was mean and cruel, even at Christmas. At the end of the story, Scrooge saw that he was wrong, and started to be kinder to people. This book made a lot of people want to give to the poor at Christmas.

This is a picture from *A Christmas Carol.* ▲

Boxing Day

Boxing Day is the day after Christmas Day. This was the day when rich Victorians gave Christmas boxes (presents) to the poor, and to some of the people who worked for them throughout the year. The presents were usually food, money or clothes. Sometimes, there were parties for poor children.

In later Victorian times, Boxing Day was an extra day off for most people. This meant that they had time to travel home to their families for the Christmas holidays.

▲ This rich woman is bringing Christmas presents to the poor.

Christmas in Other Countries

In Victorian times, Britain ruled over other countries such as India. Many British people who worked in these countries liked to have a British Christmas.

In Australia, Christmas is in the middle of the Australian summer. People who live there spend Christmas in the sun.

These men are in India. They are eating Christmas pudding for their dinner. ▲

Christmas in Church

Most Victorians went to church on Christmas morning. They either walked or went by carriage.

A church on Christmas Eve. The man is lighting the stove so that the church will be warm on Christmas morning. ▼

Decorations

Churches were usually decorated with holly and ivy. These plants are evergreens, which means that they do not lose their leaves in winter. Long ago, before people in Britain followed the Christian religion, people thought that evergreens were magical. They used them to keep evil spirits away. For Christians, holly stands for the crown of thorns that Jesus wore when he died.

Many Scottish churches were not decorated. The people did not want to celebrate Jesus' birthday with a custom which began before Christianity.

A Family Party

People decorated their homes with evergreens too. The family in the picture have hung mistletoe from the lamp, and decorated the picture frames with holly. They are having a Christmas party.

▲ This family is having a Christmas party in their home.

Christmas Carols

People used to sing carols before Queen Victoria's reign, but it was the Victorians who wrote the words of the carols down and published them. They also wrote some new Christmas carols.

◄ These people are singing a Christmas carol in church.

Carol Singers

Victorian carol singers were called waits. They visited people's houses, singing carols and playing their instruments. In return, people gave them money and sometimes a spicy hot drink.

In later Victorian times, most churches had organs instead of bands of musicians.

These waits are playing carols by the light of a lantern. ▶

The Church Service

The Christmas Day service was held at
11 o'clock in the morning.

Most people went to the Christmas Day
service, including servants if they were not
too busy cooking the Christmas dinner.

▲ This family has just come
out of church on Christmas
morning.

Food

Many Victorians did not have enough money to buy a turkey for their Christmas dinner. In the north of Britain, people often ate roast beef, and in the south they ate goose. Very poor people did not have anything special at all. On Christmas Day in 1840, Queen Victoria ate beef and roast swan.

▼ These people are collecting their Christmas dinners from the baker.

The Baker's Oven

Most poor people did not have ovens in their homes. They asked the baker to cook their meat for them. When the meat was cooked, they covered it with a lid or a cloth and took it home to eat.

◄ This woman is taking her Christmas pudding out of the copper.

Cooking the Christmas Pudding

Many people boiled their Christmas pudding in the copper. This was a big copper bowl, heated by a fire, which people used for heating water. The pudding had to be wrapped in a cloth – it looked like a cannonball.

Stirring the Christmas Pudding

Everybody stirred the Christmas pudding mixture in turn. As each person stirred, they made a wish and dropped a silver coin into the bowl.

On Christmas Day, if a person's slice of pudding had a coin in it, their wish was supposed to come true!

◄ This girl is stirring the pudding and making a wish.

Christmas Turkeys

In early Victorian times, Christmas turkeys had to walk all the way from the farm to the market in London. The journey sometimes took four months, and the turkeys wore leather boots to protect their feet.

Very rich people ate boar's head at their Christmas parties. A boar is a wild pig. This picture shows a boar's head decorated with holly. Can you see what is in the boar's mouth?

Christmas Dinner

For a rich family, Christmas dinner was a great feast. The cook and the maids cooked and served the meal. Then they did the washing up. Poor people ate their dinner in the kitchen, or even in the street outside the baker's shop.

These people are ready for their Christmas pudding. ▼

Twelfth Night Cake

Twelfth Night is on 6 January – 12 days after Christmas Day. The Victorians made special cakes. In later Victorian times, people started to make Christmas cakes instead. In Scotland, many people made shortbread.

This Twelfth Night cake was made for Queen Victoria in 1849. ▶

Cards and Decorations

Every year, people send millions of Christmas cards and birthday cards. This custom only began in Victorian times.

The First Christmas Cards

This is one of the first Christmas cards.
A thousand of these cards were printed in
1843. They were sold for a shilling (5p) each,
which was very expensive at that time.

This is a Victorian
Christmas card. ▶

New Year Cards

In early Victorian times, people sent New Year cards, like the one on the right, instead of Christmas cards.

After 1840, people could send letters or cards anywhere in Britain for a penny. This was called the Penny Post. Many people could afford this so they started to send more cards to relatives and friends.

Christmas Cards

▲ A Victorian New Year's card.

In later Victorian times, many more Christmas cards were sent. This was because:

- New printing methods made the cards cheaper.

- After 1870, people could send cards for only a halfpenny.

▲ All these Christmas cards were popular in late Victorian times.

Christmas Trees

Christmas trees were another new idea in Victorian Britain. They were already popular in Germany, and Queen Victoria had a German husband, Prince Albert. It was Prince Albert who brought the idea to Britain.

Rich people began buying Christmas trees. They decorated them with sweets, toys, fruit and candles. The servants had to make sure that the tree did not catch fire when the candles were lit.

This is the Christmas tree that Prince Albert put up in Windsor Castle in 1848. ▶

Decorations

Many Victorians made their own Christmas decorations. The one in the picture is called a kissing bough. People were supposed to kiss each other under the mistletoe.

Children made decorations from strips of coloured paper. They also made Christmas messages, cutting out paper letters and putting them together to make words.

Poor people could not afford decorations. They sometimes wrote Christmas messages in chalk round their fireplaces.

A kissing bough was a popular Christmas decoration in Victorian times. ▶

Presents

Christmas presents for children were a late Victorian idea. At the beginning of Queen Victoria's reign, only adults gave each other presents. They did this on New Year's Day. Later, they gave each other Christmas presents instead, and children were given presents too.

Toys

Children love getting toys for Christmas. In early Victorian times, toys were very expensive because they were made by hand. Later, factories started to make toys, so they became cheaper to buy.

Here are some toys and games from the 1870s. ▼

Handmade Presents

Many Victorian children made Christmas presents for their families. Magazines gave them ideas such as:

- slippers (for Grandad)
- a pincushion (for Grandma)
- mittens (for Father)
- a photograph frame (for Mother)
- a pen-wiper (for a brother)
- an apron (for a sister)

▲ These Victorian Christmas presents were made by hand.

Presents from under the Tree

Rich people put presents for the children and the servants under the Christmas tree. Servants were often given cloth to make a new dress or a new shirt.

These children are collecting their presents from under the tree. ▶

◄ This child has hung up two stockings!

Christmas Stockings

Many Victorian children hung up stockings on Christmas Eve. On Christmas morning, the stockings were full of presents.

Even poor children found an apple or an orange, a new penny and perhaps a small toy in their stockings.

Christmas Shopping

The Victorians often did their Christmas shopping from home. They sent away for presents that were advertised in newspapers and magazines. There were mail-order catalogues as well.

If presents were chosen in a shop, they could be delivered to a house by train, by carriage or by bicycle.

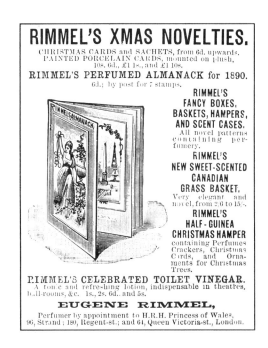

▲ This is a page from a Victorian mail-order catalogue.

Father Christmas

Ideas about Father Christmas, or Santa Claus, come from two stories.

In the first story, which is very old, Father Christmas was part of festivals held in the middle of winter in Britain. He was dressed in green as a sign of the coming spring.

The second story is about Saint Nicholas. He was called Sinter Klaas in Holland, and later, Santa Claus in the USA and Britain. He had a sleigh full of toys which was pulled by reindeer.

◄ This is a picture of Father Christmas.

Games and Treats

Television and radio had not been invented in Victorian times, so people had to entertain themselves. At Christmas time they played games, and sometimes children were taken to a pantomime.

Games

These children are playing a game called snapdragon. Brandy was poured over a bowl of currants, and the brandy was set on fire. The players had to try to snatch currants from the flames.

Do not try this game at home – it is very dangerous.

Why do you think the game was called snapdragon? ▶

More Games

Blind man's buff was another popular game. A person wore a blindfold and tried to catch another player. If a person was caught, they had to wear the blindfold next.

Charades were popular too. To play charades, someone chooses a word and acts it out without saying anything. The other players have to guess what the word is.

Christmas Crackers

A London sweet maker called Tom Smith used to roll messages round his sweets and wrap them in twists of coloured paper. In 1846, Smith had three ideas which made his sweet packets even better. He found a way of making them go bang, and then he put paper hats and small toys inside. These were the first Christmas crackers.

▲ These children are pulling a Christmas cracker.

Magic Lantern Shows

A magic lantern was a lantern with a special lens in it. If you put a glass slide with a picture on it into the lantern, you could shine the picture on to the wall. Magic lantern shows were very popular at Christmas time.

This family is enjoying a magic lantern show. ▼

Pantomimes

Pantomimes were special plays that were popular Christmas treats for rich Victorian families. The Victorian children could watch the people in the pantomime act out their favourite stories. Pantomimes usually took place on Boxing Day.

These people are watching a Christmas pantomime. ▼

Timeline

BC	AD 0		500	
		43	410 'The Dark Ages'	
Celts		Roman Britain	Anglo-Saxons	Vikings

1830–1840

1837
Victoria becomes Queen.

1840
Prince Albert puts up a Christmas tree in Windsor Castle.

1840–1850

1840
The Penny Post is introduced.

1843
A Christmas Carol, written by Charles Dickens, is published.

1843
The first Christmas cards are printed.

1846
The first Christmas cracker is pulled.

1850–1860

1851
The carol *See Amid the Winter's Snow* is published.

1860–1870

1868
The carol *O Little Town of Bethlehem* is published.

1000				1500						2000
1066				1485	1603	1714	1837	1901		

Middle Ages

Normans

Tudors · Stuarts · Georgians · Victorians · 20th Century

1870–1880

1870
The halfpenny postage rate is introduced.

1880–1890

1883
The carol *Away in a Manger* is published.

1890–1900

1898
Turkeys become popular for Christmas dinner.

1900–1910

1901
The construction toy Meccano is invented.

1901
Queen Victoria dies.

Glossary

Carol A religious song that is sung at Christmas time.

Carriage A horse-drawn cart.

Christmas pudding A pudding made with dried fruit and spices. We eat it at Christmas time.

Mail-order catalogues Magazines from which you can choose presents. The presents are then delivered to your home.

Pantomime A type of play based on a children's story.

Saints Holy people in the Christian religion.

Shilling A coin worth 12 old pennies.

Stockings Long socks made of wool. They were hung up on fireplaces at Christmas time and filled with presents.

Stove An old-fashioned word for cooker.

Waits Victorian carol singers and musicians.

Workhouses Places where people who were too old, poor or sick to look after themselves lived in Victorian times.

Books to Read

Wood, T., *Christmas*
  (A & C Black, 1991)
*Victorian Christmas Book – Press
  Out* (Dorling Kindersley, 1992)

Places to Visit

Many museums have displays about Christmas. The museums listed nearly always have a Christmas display in the winter, but telephone first to make sure.

England
County Durham: North of England
  Open Air Museum, Beamish,
  DH9 0RG. Tel. 01207 231811
Derbyshire: Sudbury Hall, Sudbury.
  Tel: 01283 585305

Humberside: Cusworth Hall,
  Cusworth Lane, Doncaster,
  Humberside. Tel: 01302 782342
London: Museum of Childhood,
  Cambridge Heath Road, London,
  E2 9PA. Tel: 0181 9802415
  Geffrye Museum, Kingsland Road,
  London, E2 8EA.
  Tel: 0171 7399893
  Victoria and Albert Museum,
  Cromwell Road, South
  Kensington, London, SW7 2RL.
  Tel: 0171 9388500

Scotland
Lothian: Museum of Childhood,
  High Street, Edinburgh.
  Tel: 0131 5294142

Wales
Gwynedd: Museum of Childhood,
  Castle Street, Beaumaris.
  Tel: 01248 810448

Index

A Christmas Carol 6
Australia 7

baker's oven 13
Boxing Day 7, 27

Christmas
   cards 4, 16–17
   carols 10
   crackers 26
   Day 5, 6, 8, 11, 12, 22
   Eve 8, 22
   pudding 7, 13–14
   services 6, 11
   stockings 22
   trees 18

decorations 8, 9, 19
   kissing bough 19
   mistletoe 9, 19

England 5
evergreens 8, 9

Father Christmas 4, 23
festivals 4

games 5, 24–25
   blind man's buff 25
   charades 25
   snapdragon 24

India 7

Jesus 4, 8

magic lantern shows 26
mail-order catalogues 23
meat 12–13, 14

pantomimes 27
Penny Post 17
presents 4, 5, 6, 7, 20–23
   toys 20
Prince Albert 18

saints' days 4
Scotland 5, 8, 15

turkeys 14
Twelfth Night cake 15

waits 10
Wales 5